THE BASIC

BIBLE
POCKET
GUIDE

JIM GEORGE

HARVEST HOUSE PUBLISHERS
EUGENE, OREGON

Cover by Dugan Design Group

THE BASIC BIBLE POCKET GUIDE
Copyright © 2016 Jim George
Published by Harvest House Publishers
Eugene, Oregon 97402
www.harvesthousepublishers.com

ISBN 978-0-7369-6447-0 (pbk.)
ISBN 978-0-7369-6448-7 (eBook)

Printed in the United States of America

15 16 17 18 19 20 21 22 / DP-JH / 10 9 8 7 6 5 4 3 2 1

Welcome to
The Basic Bible Pocket Guide

This pocket guide provides quick summaries of all 66 books of the Bible. As you read these summaries, you will discover the main message God intended for His readers in each book of the Bible, as well as a "life message" just for you.

From a big-picture standpoint, the Bible is divided into two major sections:

The Old Testament

The Old Testament is a collection of 39 books, which break down into these main categories:

History—The first 17 books (Genesis through Esther) give the history of creation through the inception and destruction of the nation of Israel.

Poetry—The next five books (Job through Song of Solomon) use Hebrew poetry to delve into the questions of suffering, wisdom, life, love, and most importantly, the character and nature of God.

Prophecy—The last 17 books (Isaiah through Malachi) were written by men appointed to "speak" for God. Their messages were to entreat and warn God's people that continued disobedience would lead to disaster. In the midst of these dire warnings was a clear ray of hope that the coming Messiah would make things right.

The New Testament

Like the Old Testament, the New Testament is not one book, but a collection of 27 individual books that reflect a wide range of themes, literary forms, and purposes.

History—The first five books (Matthew through Acts) record the life and times of Jesus, the Messiah who was prophesied in the Old Testament. Acts gives the record of the spread of the good news of Jesus' offer of salvation, beginning with Jerusalem and going to the outermost parts of the earth.

Doctrine—The last 22 books (Romans through Revelation) contain letters of teaching and instruction in Christian truth and practice.

A Personal Word

It is my hope that *The Basic Bible Pocket Guide* will...

— become a useful tool to help you study the Bible,

— better acquaint you with God's singular message of salvation for mankind, and

— stimulate you to understand the amazing and life-changing truths in God's Word.

Genesis

*In the beginning God
created the heavens and the earth. (1:1)*

Theme: Beginnings
Date written: 1445–1405 BC
Author: Moses
Setting: Middle East

GENESIS is about beginnings. God begins the Bible, His written revelation, with major events such as the creation of the universe, the fall of man into sin, the flood of judgment, and the founding of the nation of Israel. In the book of Genesis, God also introduces readers to the individual people who will be part of His plan for redeeming the human race.

LIFE APPLICATION: Just as with key players in the book of Genesis—Abraham, Jacob, Joseph, and others—God can do great things through weak vessels, and that includes you. This is one of the wonderful messages of the book of Genesis: The God who created us is not finished with us. He is in the business of "re-creating" us, giving us new beginnings and helping us become the kind of people He desires us to be. By His grace and because of His sovereign plan, your mistakes and shortcomings do not disqualify you from being part of His grand plan, a plan still being worked out in you. God is well able to turn your tragedies into triumphs. Whatever your past, and whatever your failures, make this a day of beginnings—starting with reading your Bible.

Prayer: Lord, You showed the men and women of Genesis grace and mercy, and I thank You for extending that same grace and mercy to me.

God uses the flawed and the imperfect to accomplish His perfect will.

Exodus

*I have come down to deliver them out
of the hand of the Egyptians,
and to bring them up from that land
to a good and large land… (3:8)*

Theme: Deliverance
Date written: 1445–1405 BC
Author: Moses
Setting: From Egypt to Mount Sinai

EXODUS is about deliverance. After being slaves for 400 years, God delivered His chosen people from slavery. Pharaoh refused Moses' request that the Israelites be allowed to leave Egypt, and God sent ten dramatic and miraculous plagues to convince Pharaoh to let the people go. The last plague was the death of the Egyptian firstborn, whereas the Israelite firstborn were preserved through the Passover lamb's blood sprinkled on the doorposts of each Israelite home. At this point Pharaoh finally allowed for the massive, wondrous exodus. But it was difficult for the Israelites to adjust to freedom. Slavery in Egypt had its benefits, and God's people often looked back on their days of slavery with lustful longing, forgetting that they had been treated inhumanely.

LIFE APPLICATION: As He did with the Israelites, God extends deliverance to you from slavery—slavery to sin—through the shed blood of God's perfect lamb, the Lord Jesus Christ. But, like the Israelites, you are often tempted to look back, longing for the pleasures of sin while forgetting the harsh cruelty of living under sin's bondage. Let Exodus remind you of your deliverance through the blood of Jesus. Keep looking forward! Keep remembering the glory of God and His Son's victory over sin—including your sin.

Prayer: Lord, help me to always remember the glory of Your Son's victory over sin—my sin.

God hears the cries of His suffering people and delivers them.

Leviticus

I am the LORD your God...
You shall be holy; for I am holy. (11:44)

Theme: Instruction
Date written: 1445–1405 BC
Author: Moses
Setting: Mount Sinai

LEVITICUS is about instruction. One year has gone by since God's people left Egypt. During that year, two new developments have taken place in God's dealings with His people. First, God's glory is now residing among the Israelites; and second, a central place of worship—the tabernacle—exists. But it was apparent that the people had very little knowledge of how to worship and live God's way. God used His servant Moses to deliver His Word to instruct the people how to live holy in response to the holiness of God. This emphasis on the holiness and character of God is repeated more than 50 times through the phrases "I am the LORD" and "I am Holy."

LIFE APPLICATION: Whether you realize it or not, your Christian perspectives are being challenged or distorted by the culture around you. Your worship and morality are constantly being influenced—or informed, fashioned, or forged—by an ungodly society. But God gives you His instruction book, the Bible, to correct any warped values and teach you how to properly live and worship. Be careful not to disregard God's instructions. Read your Bible so that you understand what a holy God demands for holy living. Always heed God's instruction.

Prayer: Lord, give me the discipline I need to daily read Your Word so I can be influenced daily to live a holy life.

You are being fashioned into one of two images—either God's, or the world's. Make a choice!

Numbers

*These are the journeys of the children of Israel,
who went out of the land of Egypt by their
armies under the hand of Moses
and Aaron. (33:1)*

Theme: Journeys
Date written: 1445–1405 BC
Author: Moses
Setting: The wilderness

NUMBERS is about journeys. Before Israel could enter their Promised Land, 12 spies were sent into the land to determine the strength of the enemy. Ten of the spies give a very fearful and negative report, saying there was no way that the land could be conquered. This negative report affected the entire army. They focused on the size of their enemy rather than on the size and greatness of their God. The consequence of their unbelief? God's people had to wander for 40 years in the wilderness before entering the Promised Land. Written in the final year of Moses' life, the book of Numbers concentrates on events surrounding the 12 spies and the people's unwillingness to enter the land, and on the fortieth year of wandering, just before a new generation would enter the Promised Land. This journey of 40 years records the experiences of two generations of the nation of Israel.

LIFE APPLICATION: Only two spies gave a positive report because they focused on God's power and His promises. When you are faced with challenges, learn a lesson from Joshua and Caleb and respond in faith. Focus positively on God's power rather than negatively on the problems at hand. Yes, the enemy is powerful, but God is *all*-powerful!

Prayer: Lord, Give me eyes of faith that even when the odds are overwhelming, I will believe in Your promises.

Beware of the unbelief of others. It's contagious!

Deuteronomy

What does the LORD your God require of you,
but to fear the LORD your God,
to walk in all His ways… (10:12)

Theme: Obedience
Date written: 1445–1405 BC
Author: Moses
Setting: The plains of Moab

DEUTERONOMY is about obedience. Israel was encamped east of the Jordan River across from the walled city of Jericho. It had been 40 years since the Israelites exited Egypt. The book records the verbal communication of God's divine revelation that Moses had received over the past 39-plus years of wilderness wanderings. His audience is the new generation that needs instruction in order to prepare them for entering the Promised Land. Deuteronomy reveals much about the character and nature of God. How fortunate the world is to have this written testimony of God's expectations of His creation. Moses, the leader of God's people, would not enter the Promised Land, but before he dies, he faithfully reminds the people that God's holiness requires that He honor obedience and punish disobedience.

LIFE APPLICATION: Moses' instructions concerning the character of God are still appropriate today. Learning about God will aid you in your love for Him and your pursuit of personal holiness. God is the standard. He is holy, and He expects holy behavior from His people. As a Christian, you are called to be holy as God is holy. You are called to "love" Him in obedience "with all your heart, with all your soul, and with all your strength" (Deuteronomy 6:5).

Prayer: Dear Lord, thank You for Your standard of holiness, which is stated in the Bible. By your grace, help me to live up to that standard.

Review God's Word regularly—
it will guide your steps.

Joshua

As for me and my house,
we will serve the LORD. (24:15)

Theme: Conquest
Date written: 1405–1385 BC
Author: Joshua
Setting: Canaan, the Promised Land

JOSHUA describes the conquest and settlement of the Promised Land. When Moses passed the baton of leadership on to Joshua (Deuteronomy 34), Israel was at the end of its 40 years of wilderness wanderings. Joshua had been Moses' faithful apprentice for most of those 40 years and was approaching 90 years of age when Moses called him to become Israel's new leader. Joshua's task was to lead Israel into the land of Canaan, drive out the inhabitants, and divide the land among the 12 tribes.

God's first task for Joshua as the new leader was to conquer Jericho through what sounded like a foolish plan—walk around the city of Jericho, blow trumpets, and shout. The people followed God's instructions, and the walls miraculously fell down. This task was a test to see if the people would recognize that a successful conquest would always come from God's power and not from their own abilities.

LIFE APPLICATION: The book of Joshua teaches that when it comes to fighting the battles of life and gaining spiritual victory, blessing comes through obedience to God's commands. Active faith does not require that you understand all or any of what God is doing in your life, or why. Submit to God's direction. Then watch the walls of your seemingly impossible problems miraculously come tumbling down.

Prayer: Lord, even though I don't always understand, help me to obey Your Word and reap the blessings of that obedience.

*Victory occurs when you let God
fight your battles.*

Judges

*When the children of Israel cried out to the LORD
the LORD raised up a deliverer... (3:9)*

Theme: Deliverance
Date written: about 1043 BC
Author: Samuel
Setting: Canaan

JUDGES bears the fitting name *Judges*, which refers to 12 unique leaders God graciously raised up to deliver His people when they were oppressed as a result of their disobedience. Judges is a tragic sequel to the book of Joshua. In Joshua, the people were obedient to God and enjoyed victory in their conquest of the land. In Judges, however, they were disobedient, idolatrous, and often defeated and oppressed. The final verse of Judges (21:25) gives the key to understanding this period of the history of Israel: "Everyone did what was right in his own eyes." And yet even with the widespread idolatry, immorality, and violence in Israel, God was ever faithful to deliver the people. In His gracious love, God continued to forgive them every time they cried out to Him.

LIFE APPLICATION: How often can it be said that you "do what is right in your own eyes"? It's easy to act in foolishness, ingratitude, stubbornness, and rebellion. Then you wonder why you suffer and live in utter defeat. The God of Judges is still the same God today. And, as then, so now: When you cry out to God in repentance, He is always nearby to faithfully forgive and deliver you. Are you living in spiritual defeat? Cry out to God. He is ready to send His deliverance!

Prayer: Lord, I thank You that my hope rests in knowing that You are always nearby to deliver me from spiritual defeat.

Don't compromise with the Word—
it leads to defeat.

Ruth

*Your people shall be my people,
and your God, my God. (1:16)*

Theme: Redemption
Date written: about 1030–1010 BC
Author: Unknown/possibly Samuel
Setting: Moab and Bethlehem

RUTH is about redemption. The book of Ruth was named after a young Moabite woman who tragically lost her husband, but willingly forsook her god, culture, and people and chose to follow her mother-in-law, Naomi, back to Israel. Because of Ruth's faithfulness to follow the God of Israel, she received great blessings not only for herself, but also for Naomi. Ruth's godly behavior in the midst of widespread ungodliness attracted the attention of a righteous man named Boaz. Through the ancient practice of acting as a kinsman-redeemer, Boaz offered to take the place of her dead husband. As a result, Ruth married Boaz and had a son who ultimately placed her and her son in the family line of Jesus Christ.

LIFE APPLICATION: In this Old Testament book are two great pictures. First, through Ruth, God provides an example of godly character in the midst of an ungodly world. Second, this small book illustrates the work of Christ in the New Testament. Like Boaz, the kinsman-redeemer of Ruth, Jesus is related to you by His physical birth, is able to pay the price of your redemption, and is willing to redeem you. Like Ruth, you must choose to accept Christ's offer of redemption.

Prayer: Father, I choose Jesus—my Kinsman-Redeemer—and His offer to redeem me so I can live forever in His presence in heaven.

Character takes a lifetime to develop,
but can be lost in a moment through
a foolish action.

1 Samuel

*Behold, to obey is better than
sacrifice… (15:22)*

Theme: Transition
Date written: 930–722 BC
Author: Unknown
Setting: The struggling nation of Israel

1 SAMUEL is about the transition of the 12 very individual tribes of Israel into a unified nation under one king. The book can be divided into thirds with regard to three prominent personalities—Samuel, Saul, and David. Just as Israel was in transition, so were these three men. In spite of the changes that happened to and around Samuel, he never faltered in his faithfulness to God and His people. By contrast, Saul's transition from commoner to king was marked by pride, deceit, and a progressively unrepentant heart.

LIFE APPLICATION: Whether you realize it or not, your life is in a constant state of change. Therefore you must recognize how crucial it is to make transitions well. And remember, it's not the transition itself that's critical, but how you respond to the changes that come your way. How can you make sure your life and attitudes honor God with each change that comes? Like Samuel, you choose to stay faithful and close to God through prayer and the study of His Word. Then, when a transition occurs, you will be prepared to draw on God's strength and honor Him with your godly attitudes and actions.

Prayer: Lord, when a transition comes my way, help me to draw on Your strength to ensure I handle the change properly.

*It's not how you start that's important,
but how well you finish.*

2 Samuel

*Your house and your kingdom
shall be established forever... (7:16)*

Theme: Unification
Date written: 931–722 BC
Author: Unknown
Setting: United kingdom of Israel

2 SAMUEL picks up where 1 Samuel leaves off. Saul was gone, and David was declared king and reigned in Jerusalem for 40 years. David's adultery with another man's wife and the subsequent deliberate killing of her husband marked the turning point in the life and success of David. God was displeased. After being confronted for his sin, David realized his need to make things right with God through a repentant heart. Unfortunately, his repentance couldn't repair the damage brought about by his sin. Yes, he was forgiven. And yes, his relationship with God was restored. But the list of those who suffered from and because of David's sins was a long and tragic one. From this point onward, David experienced continual struggles both within his family and with the nation.

LIFE APPLICATION: In spite of his shortcomings, David remained a man after God's own heart. Why? Obviously it wasn't because David lived a sinless life. Far from that! He often failed in his personal life, but when he did so, he eventually turned back to God in repentance and restored his ongoing relationship with Him. Do you desire to be a man or a woman after God's own heart? Realize that God isn't looking for perfection; rather, He is looking for progression. When you stumble and fall, be quick to ask God for forgiveness and keep on progressing in your faith.

Prayer: Thank You for seeing me as a work in progress. Help me to be quick to recognize my sins and seek Your forgiveness.

> *Blessing comes to you when you are*
> *obedient to God's commands,*
> *and trouble when you aren't.*

1 Kings

Because you... have not kept
My covenant and My statutes...
I will surely tear the kingdom
away from you... (11:11)

Theme: Disruption
Date written: 561–538 BC
Author: Unknown
Setting: Israel

1 KINGS describes how, at the height of Israel's affluence and influence, the tiny nation was plunged into poverty and paralysis—all because the people had turned away from God. The failures started after Solomon, David's son, stopped applying the wisdom God had granted him, and turned his heart to following the false religions of his many wives. Solomon's son, Rehoboam, took bad advice from his foolish friends—advice that resulted in the split of the kingdom.

LIFE APPLICATION: God has provided you with many avenues for obtaining wisdom and averting failure. Resist your inclination to accept advice with easy solutions and reject help that would require a more difficult path. Don't bypass God's resources, which can help ensure that your decisions honor Him and bless others. In other words, godly advice will keep you from failure.

Prayer: Thank You, Lord, for Your Word, the Spirit, and the wisdom of others to help me in my decision-making process.

Wisdom must be applied daily;
don't move ahead on anything without it.

2 Kings

*I will also remove Judah from My sight,
as I have removed Israel... (23:27)*

Theme: Dispersion
Date written: 561–538 BC
Author: Unknown
Setting: Divided kingdom of Israel and Judah

2 KINGS is about dispersion. The book continues, without a break, to record the history of the kingdoms of Israel to the north and Judah to the south. Even with repeated warnings from God's prophetic messengers, the leaders and people in both kingdoms refused to obey God. They threw themselves headlong toward a collision course with captivity. As a result, God allowed the Assyrians to conquer the northern kingdom and the Babylonians to take the southern kingdom. The people were taken captive into exile, and the glory of the once-united kingdom faded away.

LIFE APPLICATION: Even though 1 and 2 Kings are two separate books in today's Bibles, they were originally one and they shared the same theme: When the kings followed God's covenant ways, they and their people prospered; but those kings who refused to obey God were sure to face judgment. The split kingdoms provide a perfect example of what happens when you adopt the ways of the godless. Instead of adopting their ways, turn from them and humbly call upon God. Nurture a heart of contrition. Seek God's ways by turning from any practices that are displeasing to Him. This is the path of forgiveness and blessing!

Prayer: "Search me, O God, and know my heart...and see if there is any wicked way in me, and lead me in the way everlasting" (Psalm 139:23-24).

*An idol is anything that you regard
more highly than God.*

1 Chronicles

David knew that the LORD
had established him as king over Israel,
for his kingdom was highly exalted... (14:2)

Theme: Israel's spiritual history
Date written: 450–430 BC
Author: Ezra
Setting: Israel after the captivity

1 CHRONICLES is about Israel's religious history. The books of 1 and 2 Chronicles were originally one book in the Hebrew Bible. They were divided at the time of their translation from the Hebrew. First Chronicles covers the same period of Israel's history as the book of 2 Samuel but with one difference—2 Samuel gives a political history of the Davidic dynasty, while 1 Chronicles gives the religious history until David's death. This book was written after the 70-year captivity in Babylon so the returning exiles could review the purpose of the temple as well as the roles of the law and priesthood. First Chronicles was to provide a spiritual history lesson intended to help the returnees to remember the consequence of sin.

LIFE APPLICATION: A review of your spiritual history and God's eternal promises is an important reason for you to read your Bible. God's promises regarding your eternal destiny are available in Scripture for your constant review. Just as God was faithful to His people in the past by bringing them out of captivity, you can rely on Him to be faithful in the present by protecting and providing for you. As you remember who you are in Christ, you can look ahead with confidence, knowing that God will provide for you and all future generations of believers until His return.

Prayer: Lord, I have a short memory when it comes to sin. Remind me often of the great price You paid for my salvation.

*Your past mistakes provide lessons for
your present holiness.*

2 Chronicles

If My people... will humble themselves,
and pray and seek My face,
and turn from their wicked way,
then I will hear from heaven,
and will forgive their sin and
heal their land. (7:14)

Theme: Israel's spiritual heritage
Date written: 450–430 BC
Author: Ezra
Setting: Israel after the exile

2 CHRONICLES is about remembrance—the same theme as 1 Chronicles. Upon their return from captivity, the exiles were to remember the temple as well as the roles that the law and the priesthood played in their lives. The two books of Chronicles look back to Israel's former glory and offer encouragement as the people rebuild their heritage. Starting with the time of King Solomon, this is a spiritual chronicle of David's lineage, with the wicked kings of the northern kingdom and their history being completely omitted.

LIFE APPLICATION: Like Israel, you are placed on this earth to represent God. But, again like Israel, it's easy to forget who you are and stumble blindly after the idols of wealth, prestige, and fleshly self-fulfillment. If you make anything a higher priority than God, you are worshipping it and not God, despite what you might profess with your lips. The people of Israel did not heed the warnings of God's prophets, and they experienced God's judgment. Don't wait for God's hand of discipline; examine your heart and put away any distraction to a wholehearted worship of Him.

Prayer: Lord, examine my heart and expose any distraction to a wholehearted worship of You.

God intends that your failures be stepping stones, not stumbling blocks.

Ezra

*I was encouraged,
as the hand of the LORD my God
was upon me... (7:28)*

Theme: Restoration
Date written: 457–444 BC
Author: Ezra
Setting: Jerusalem

EZRA is about restoration. Ezra, the author of 1 and 2 Chronicles, picks up where he left off at the end of 2 Chronicles. The first six chapters of the book that bears Ezra's name record the account of the return of the first group of exiles under the leadership of a man named Zerubbabel, a direct descendant of King David. Their task was to restore the altar and religious feast and lay the foundation for a new temple. Chapters 7 through 10 record the return of the second group of exiles under the leadership of Ezra. As a priest and teacher, Ezra was to rebuild the people spiritually and morally.

The primary message of this book is that God orchestrated all of what happened during their past grim captivity and would continue to work with the returning exiles to give hope.

LIFE APPLICATION: Just as God restored His chosen people from their captivity, He continues to show His mercy and grace to each new generation of His people, including yours. No matter how difficult your present "captivity" or trial, you are never far removed from God's love and mercy. Restoration is available each time when you return to Him.

Prayer: Thank You, Lord, that whether I feel it or not, Your hand is always upon me.

*God is at work behind the scenes to
lead and direct your life.*

Nehemiah

*Then I said to them, "You see the distress
that we are in, how Jerusalem lies waste,
and its gates are burned with fire.
Come and let us build the wall of Jerusalem,
that we may no longer be a reproach." (2:17)*

Theme: Reconstruction
Date written: 424–400 BC
Author: Nehemiah
Setting: Jerusalem

NEHEMIAH provides a sequel to the narrative of
the book of Ezra and is about rebuilding the wall
around Jerusalem. Ezra was concerned with the
need to rebuild the temple and restore the worship of God. Nehemiah, in turn, was concerned
with rebuilding the wall and instructing the people in the law. In the midst of the building project,
Nehemiah faced overwhelming opposition from
God's enemies, who over the past 90 years had suc-
cessfully blocked other attempts to restore the wall.
Yet from the day Nehemiah understood his part in
God's plan, his trust in God's provision and protection was unwavering. And as a result, even in the
midst of the opposition and difficulties, his trust in

God inspired others toward confidence in God as well, and the wall was completed in just 52 days!

LIFE APPLICATION: When it comes to the building or rebuilding of your spiritual life, follow the example of Nehemiah and remember that God's Word should be foundational to your every move. How important is Scripture when you make decisions? Where does God's truth fit into your building plans? If you want to build a better life, look to God's blueprint, the Bible.

Prayer: Lord, help me understand the part I play in Your plan. Then give me strength to trust in Your provision and protection so that I don't waver in fulfilling Your purpose.

Most of what you do to fulfill God's purposes will require acts of faith.

Esther

Yet who knows
whether you have come to the kingdom
for such a time as this? (4:14)

Theme: Preservation
Date written: 450–431 BC
Author: Unknown
Setting: The court of Persia

ESTHER is about preservation. While Ezra and Nehemiah deal with the remnant of Jews who returned to Israel, the book of Esther deals with the Jews who decided to stay in the land of their captivity. Esther is one of two books in the Bible given a woman's name, the other being Ruth. Esther is the story of a young Jewish woman without parents who became queen of the vast Persian Empire. In the midst of a desperate and seemingly hopeless crisis, this young woman exerted her influence, and the Jewish people were saved from annihilation.

LIFE APPLICATION: Esther did not choose to be in the king's palace nor to be his queen. But in her position there, God used her mightily to preserve His people. Regardless of what you have or don't have, whether your circumstances are considered good or bad, God can and will protect you. And He can and will use you to help His people. You may not see His mighty hand of provision or protection, but be assured, He is at work on your behalf. He is your ultimate security and provider, and He will take care of you.

Don't let less-than-perfect circumstances keep you from trusting God. And don't let a difficult life prevent you from serving God.

Prayer: Dear Lord, give me the courage to speak up for my beliefs and be willing to suffer the consequences.

> *God's people—including you—*
> *have been prepared by God for*
> *"such a time as this"!*

Job

*I abhor myself,
and repent in dust and ashes. (42:6)*

Theme: Blessings through suffering
Date written: 2000–1800 BC
Author: Unknown
Setting: Land of Uz

JOB is about the problem of suffering. The book of Job is considered by many Bible scholars to be the oldest book in the Bible. Job probably lived during the same time period as Abraham. Like Abraham, Job was a wealthy and upright man who feared God. This book that bears Job's name, describes the death of his self-righteousness as he and a group of his friends struggled with the reasons behind his sufferings.

Job is a fascinating story of riches-to-rags-to-riches. It provides insights into the problem of suffering, the certainty of divine sovereignty, the activities of Satan, and a faith that persists. Job was tested, and his faith endured because it was built on the firm foundation of God.

LIFE APPLICATION: God is all-wise and all-powerful, and His will is perfect. However, our finite minds don't always understand His actions. Suffering usually doesn't make sense to us. We question God, and at times we are tempted to shake our fist at Him in frustration. Job teaches that there are many things we will never understand, including suffering. But there is one thing we can know: God is never insensitive to our problems. His sufficiency makes up for our insufficiency, and, in the end, we are drawn closer to Him.

Prayer: God, I know You always have a reason for what You are asking me to endure. Help me to resist asking, "Why?" and instead, to ask, "What? What do You want me to learn from what's happening in my life?"

God's sufficiency makes up for your insufficiency.

Psalms

My mouth shall speak the praise of the LORD,
and all flesh shall bless
His holy name forever and ever. (145:21)

Theme: Praise
Date written: 1410–450 BC
Author: Various authors
Setting: Heaven and earth

PSALMS is about worship and praise. The Psalms are poetic expressions of human and religious feelings, and are divided into five sections or "books" that comprise a total of 150 individual psalms. The Psalms span the ten centuries from Moses to the days after the Jewish people's exile. They consist of a wide variety of styles and purposes and emotions, such as lament, thanksgiving, praise, worship, pilgrimage, petition, and penitence. Even though the psalms were written by different authors over the course of hundreds of years, they are wonderfully unified by their common theme of worship and praise of God for who He is, what He has done, and what He will do in the future.

LIFE APPLICATION: The Psalms focus on God and reflect His plans for His people. The more you read them, the more you understand and are blessed by what you learn of God and His work as Creator, Redeemer, Sustainer, and Comforter. Like the psalmist, you should be moved to praise and worship the Lord.

— If you need a handbook for praise and worship, read Psalms.
— If you need to better understand God, read Psalms.
— If you need a source of comfort in times of pain and distress, read Psalms.
— If you need a guide for your ongoing relationship with God, read Psalms.

Prayer: Lord, I thank You that when I feel distant and removed from Your presence, all I have to do is pick up a Bible and read a psalm and have my relationship with You revitalized.

Do you desire a deeper and more meaningful relationship with God? Read Psalms!

Proverbs

The fear of the LORD
is the beginning of knowledge,
but fools despise wisdom and
instruction. (1:7)

Theme: Practical wisdom
Date written: 971–686 BC
Author: Primarily Solomon
Setting: Everyday life

PROVERBS is about practical wisdom. While David is the author of a majority of the psalms, his son, Solomon, is the author of most of the book of Proverbs. Solomon came to the throne with great promise. God granted him wisdom beyond that of any other man of his day. In his earlier life, Solomon was sought out for his wisdom and practical advice. Unfortunately, in his later years, Solomon failed to live out the truths he knew and wrote about. He became the fool that he so ardently taught against in Proverbs.

LIFE APPLICATION: As you read Proverbs, understand well Solomon's message that knowing God is the key to wisdom. "The fear of the LORD is the beginning of wisdom, and the knowledge of the Holy One is understanding" (Proverbs 9:10). Then read the rest of God's Word to gain more of God's wisdom. Listen to the thoughts and lessons from not only the world's wisest man, Solomon, but also from the Bible's many other teachers. Here's what you will learn by reading Proverbs, which will lead you into making right decisions.

— Choose your words carefully. They reveal your inner character.
— Choose to work diligently. You will profit and gain skills, and God will be honored.
— Choose your friends carefully. They are a reflection of you.
— Choose moral character and devotion to God. This is success in God's eyes.

Prayer: Lord, help me learn a most important lesson from the life of Solomon: It's not so much how well I start that matters, but how I finish.

To grow in wisdom, read your Bible repeatedly and apply its truths faithfully.

Ecclesiastes

*Fear God and keep His commandments,
for this is man's all. (12:13)*

Theme: All is vanity apart from God
Date written: 940–931 BC
Author: Solomon
Setting: The end of Solomon's life

ECCLESIASTES is an autobiography written by King Solomon at the end of his life after he strayed away from God. It speaks of vanity apart from God. As if he were reporting the results of a scientific experiment, Solomon "the Preacher" (1:1) shares about his search for satisfaction. In four "sermons," he relates his discovery that life without God is a long and fruitless search for enjoyment, meaning, and fulfillment. Solomon hopes to spare his readers the bitterness of learning through personal experiences that carrying out life's pursuits apart from God is empty, fruitless, and meaningless.

LIFE APPLICATION: Solomon's remarks are preserved in the book of Ecclesiastes for a purpose—to lead you to seek true happiness in God alone. Solomon is not trying to destroy all your hopes. He is instead directing your hopes to the only One who can truly fulfill them. Solomon affirms the value of knowledge, relationships, work, and pleasure. However, he also shows their proper place in the light of eternity and concludes, "Fear God and keep His commandments, for this is man's all" (Ecclesiastes 12:13). Here's a summary of Solomon's final understanding of life:

— Only in God can you find real fulfillment. Nothing in this life will bring true meaning and happiness apart from God.
— True happiness comes only from obedience to God.
— Life without God is a long and fruitless search for enjoyment, meaning, and fulfillment.

Prayer: Dear Lord, may my life's focus be to honor You and keep Your commandments. May this be my daily commitment to You!

All your life should be measured in
the light of eternity.

Song of Solomon

My beloved is mine, and I am his. (2:16)

Theme: Love and marriage
Date written: 971–965 BC
Author: Solomon
Setting: Early in Solomon's reign

SONG OF SOLOMON is about love and marriage. A youthful King Solomon is writing a wedding song to describe his love for and marriage to a beautiful country girl referred to as "the Shulamite." This song records the dialogue between an ordinary Jewish maiden and her "beloved," the king of Israel. Solomon's tender poetic marriage song gives us God's perspective on love, sex, and marriage. This book of inspired poetry gives you a model of God's intentions for love and marriage. It celebrates the joy and intimacy that make up a romantic relationship between a husband and wife.

LIFE APPLICATION: Love is a powerful, God-given expression of feeling and commitment between two people. Love doesn't just look for outward physical beauty. It looks for the inner qualities that never fade with time—spiritual commitment, integrity, sensitivity, and sincerity. Therefore, such love is not to be regarded in a casual manner, and the physical expression of this kind of true love should be withheld until marriage. And after marriage, it is this genuine, internal love that won't let any walls come between you and your spouse.

God takes great joy in the passionate romantic love between a husband and wife. A couple should openly express their love and admiration for each other. A husband and wife honor God when they do that.

Prayer: Dear God, thank You for this reminder that Your steadfast and unceasing love for me is modeled in the love relationship between a husband and wife. May I demonstrate my love for You by fulfilling Your will for my life.

Marriage, with all its misunderstandings,
is a work in progress.

Isaiah

All we like sheep have gone astray;
we have turned, every one, to his own way;
and the LORD has laid on Him
the iniquity of us all. (53:6)

Theme: Salvation
Date written: 700–680 BC
Author: Isaiah
Setting: Mainly in Jerusalem

ISAIAH is about salvation. The book of Isaiah is the first of the writings of the prophets, and Isaiah himself is generally considered to be one of the greatest prophets. His ministry spanned the reigns of four kings of Judah. The basic theme of this book is found in Isaiah's name, which means "salvation is of the Lord." Isaiah pictured man as being in great need of salvation—a salvation that is of God, not man. He described God as the Supreme Ruler, the sovereign Lord of history, and man's only Savior. To accomplish this salvation God would send the Messiah, who would be both a suffering servant and a sovereign Lord. This Savior was to come out of the tribe of Judah and would accomplish redemption and restoration with universal blessing for both Jews and Gentiles in His future kingdom.

LIFE APPLICATION: The Bible warns that God's judgment is coming. Therefore, you too need a Savior. You cannot save yourself. Christ's perfect sacrifice for your sins is foretold and pictured in Isaiah. Just as the prophet foretold, 700 years later, Christ came in the flesh and paid the price for sin in His death on a Roman cross. With His resurrection, He has made possible the salvation of all those who turn from their sin and come to Him. Have you committed yourself to Him? If you have experienced His salvation, continue to be faithful and live in anticipation of His soon return.

Prayer: Thank You, Father, for faithfully keeping Your promise to send Your Son, the Lord Jesus Christ, to die for my sins.

God is trustworthy, and you can count on Him to always keep His word.

Jeremiah

*Now therefore, amend your ways and your doings,
and obey the voice of the LORD your God;
then the LORD will relent concerning the doom
that He has pronounced against you. (26:13)*

Theme: Judgment
Date written: 627–586 BC
Author: Jeremiah
Setting: Jerusalem

JEREMIAH is about judgment. It is an autobiography of Jeremiah's life and ministry during the reigns of the last five kings of Judah. Some 80 to 100 years after Isaiah's death, Jeremiah entered the prophetic scene. He was called "the weeping prophet" because of his deep sorrow over the unrepentant nation, the upcoming destruction of Jerusalem, and the exile of its people.

LIFE APPLICATION: Most people's definition of success would include the acquiring of wealth, popularity, fame, power, or accomplishments. By these standards, Jeremiah was a complete failure. For 40 years, he served as God's spokesman and passionately urged the people to return to God. And yet no one listened! He was penniless, friendless, and rejected by his family. In the world's eyes, he was a failure. But in God's eyes, he was one of the most successful people in all biblical history. Why? Because success, as seen by God, involves obedience, and acceptance or rejection by people is not to be the measure of your success. You must live a life that honors and glorifies God in spite of temptations and pressures that pull you in the direction of the world. God's approval alone should be the sole standard for your life and your service to Him.

Prayer: Dear God, give me the courage to speak up for my beliefs even though it may lead to persecution and rejection.

You must view success from God's perspective, not the world's.

Lamentations

My eyes fail with tears, my heart is troubled...
because of the destruction of the
daughter of my people... (2:11)

Theme: Lament
Date written: 586 BC
Author: Jeremiah
Setting: Jerusalem

LAMENTATIONS is about grief. In this book, the prophet Jeremiah wrote an eyewitness account of the destruction of Jerusalem using five funeral poems to express his grief. But, as in his previous book, Jeremiah, he reminded his readers that God has not and will not abandon His people. God is faithful, and His mercies continue to remain available day by day. He is faithful even when we are unfaithful. God's mercies are new every morning; great is His faithfulness (Lamentations 3:23)!

LIFE APPLICATION: Most people don't like showing their emotions, especially their tears. But what makes a person cry says a lot about the person. In Jeremiah's case, his tears were for the suffering of God's people and their rebellion against Him.

What causes you to cry? Do you weep because someone has insulted you, or because someone has insulted God? Do you cry because you have lost something that gives you pleasure, or because of spiritually lost people who refuse to turn to God? The world is filled with injustice, suffering, and rebellion against God, all of which should move you to tears and action.

Prayer: Dear Lord, give me a heart of compassion for those who are suffering. May I always remember to pray for those who are less fortunate than me.

Tears are not a sign of weakness.
They are a sign of compassion. A tearless heart is
a callous heart.

Ezekiel

*I arose and went out into the plain,
and behold, the glory of the LORD stood there,
like the glory which I saw by the River
Chebar; and I fell on my face. (3:23)*

Theme: The glory of the Lord
Date written: 590–570 BC
Author: Ezekiel
Setting: Babylon

EZEKIEL is about the glory of God. While Jeremiah was prophesying in Jerusalem that the city would soon fall to the Babylonians, Ezekiel was giving a similar message to the captives who were already in Babylon. Throughout the book of Ezekiel, Ezekiel described his encounters with God's glory—His heavenly glory, His earthly glory in the temple of the past, and His glory in the temple predicted for the future. Throughout his messages, Ezekiel emphasized again and again God's declaration that all the things to come were going to happen so that people would know "that I am the LORD" (see, for example, Ezekiel 36:11,23).

LIFE APPLICATION: God's glory is visible to anyone who is willing to look up at the heavens (see Psalm 19:1). His glory is visible in His preservation of His covenant people and their promised restoration. His glory is visible in His grace toward repentant sinners during this church age. God is gloriously to be praised and worshipped. The very thought of His glory should drive you to make the changes in your life that help you to better reflect His holy nature.

Prayer: Dear heavenly Father, I take great comfort in knowing that You sovereignly control every detail of my life and that You have a purpose for me. Help me be faithful to that purpose.

If God didn't have control of all,
He couldn't be God of all.

Daniel

*The Most High God rules in the kingdom of men,
and appoints over it whomever He chooses. (5:21)*

Theme: The sovereignty of God
Date written: 530 BC
Author: Daniel
Setting: Babylon

DANIEL is about the sovereignty of God. All
through the book, Daniel repeatedly emphasized
the sovereignty and power of God over human
affairs. Daniel, an exile himself, wrote to encourage the exiled Jews by revealing God's sovereign
program for Israel during and after the period of
Gentile domination—the "times of the Gentiles"
(Luke 21:24). In spite of his surroundings, Daniel
lived a godly life and exercised tremendous influence in three kingdoms—Babylon, Media, and
Persia. As a result of his stellar character, God gave
him a view of the future rivaled only by the apostle
John's visions in the book of Revelation.

LIFE APPLICATION: During his many years as a
captive, Daniel could have despaired. He could
have thought God had abandoned him. He could

have cried, "Where is God?" Instead of giving in or giving up, this courageous man held fast to his faith in God. Daniel understood that, despite his circumstances, God was sovereign and was working out His plans for nations, kings, and individuals.

Daniel is an inspiring example of integrity for us—he lived a godly life under less-than-ideal circumstances and in an ungodly world. Be faithful in your study of God's Word. Sustain your prayer life. And maintain your integrity. Then, like Daniel, you will have a marked influence on those around you.

Prayer: Dear God, may I follow Daniel's example and live a godly life in an ungodly world. Give me the strength to be uncompromising in my obedience to Your Word.

Integrity never goes out of style.

Hosea

I will have mercy on her who had not obtained mercy;
then I will say to those who were not My people, "You are My people!"
And they shall say, "You are my God!" (2:23)

Theme: Unfaithfulness
Date written: 755–715 BC
Author: Hosea
Setting: Northern kingdom

HOSEA is about unfaithfulness and is the first of a series of 12 prophetic books called the Minor Prophets—not because they are less important, but primarily because of the lengths of these books. Each of the Minor Prophets is named after its author. The book of Hosea details the unhappy domestic union of a man and his unfaithful wife, Gomer. Their story serves as a vivid parallel of the loyalty of God and the spiritual adultery of Israel. With empathetic sorrow, Hosea, whose name means "salvation," exposed the sins of Israel and contrasted them to God's holiness. Hosea's personal suffering gave him a better understanding of God's grief over Israel's sin.

LIFE APPLICATION: Like Hosea, you too will experience times of emotional and physical suffering. However, rather than becoming bitter or giving up, you can allow God to use your suffering to comfort others in their pain. Stay loyal to God. Be faithful to Him no matter what, because He is always faithful to you.

Prayer: Dear God, I thank You that I can count on Your faithfulness even when I am not always faithful. Lord, give me the strength to resist the world's seduction and be faithful!

Repentance is the first step on the path back to your relationship with God.

Joel

Return to the LORD your God,
for He is gracious and merciful,
slow to anger, and of great kindness... (2:13)

Theme: The day of the Lord
Date written: 835–796 BC
Author: Joel
Setting: Judah/Jerusalem

JOEL is about the coming "day of the LORD" (1:15). Ever since the first sin was committed in the Garden of Eden in Genesis, man has been in rebellion against God. In Joel, the nation of Judah has taken its turn in disregarding God's laws. On behalf of God, the prophet Joel appeals to the people to repent and avert the coming disaster. Unfortunately, the people do not listen, and they will surely face their day of judgment, their "day of the LORD."

LIFE APPLICATION: No one likes to hear about God's judgment. But a holy God, not nature or the economy or anything else, is the One with whom all must reckon. People cannot ignore or offend God forever. Everyone must pay attention to God's message from His Word. If they don't, they will face the "day of the LORD." Where do you stand with God and His coming judgment? Where does Joel's message find you today? It's not too late to ask for and receive God's forgiveness. His greatest desire is for you to come to Him.

Prayer: O gracious God, I bless Your holy name and am comforted in knowing that You always give a warning before You send judgment. May I be as faithful as Joel in warning of Your coming judgment.

Judgment faces all who disregard
God's offer of salvation.

Amos

Seek good and not evil, that you may live;
so that the LORD God of hosts
will be with you... (5:14)

Theme: Punishment
Date written: 790 BC
Author: Amos
Setting: Bethel, the northern kingdom

AMOS is about punishment. This prophet offers eight pronouncements—three sermons and five visions—warning of coming disaster because of complacency, idolatry, and the oppression of the poor. Amos was not a professional prophet. He was a simple shepherd—a country boy. But he was divinely commissioned by God to bring a harsh message of judgment to the northern kingdom of Israel. However, because of the peace and prosperity Israel was experiencing at the time, Amos's message fell on deaf ears.

LIFE APPLICATION: Amos's life and prophecies have two messages:

Message #1—God hates the hypocrisy of those who say they love Him yet live excessive, indulgent lifestyles. Prosperity can easily blind you of compassion for the less fortunate.

Message #2—God uses the untrained to serve Him. You don't have to be professionally trained to speak up for God and do something when you see human injustice or sinful behavior, especially by those who claim to be Christians. You only have to follow Amos's example and answer God's call to be a testimony of righteous living.

Prayer: Dear Lord, I know at times I become complacent in my love for You and realize that this lukewarm attitude can surface almost without notice. Check my heart and renew my spirit daily.

Hypocrisy is a mask that may help you fool others, but you won't fool God.

Obadiah

No survivor shall remain of the
house of Esau. (Verse 18)

Theme: Righteous judgment
Date written: 850–840 BC
Author: Obadiah
Setting: Jerusalem/Edom

OBADIAH was written to the nation of Edom, a people who were blood relatives of those who lived in Judah and should have come to their aid. But because they reacted with indifference, God sent—through Obadiah—a message of coming disaster.

LIFE APPLICATION: Obadiah provided a clear warning that God judges those who harm His children or aid in their harm. If you are a child of God through Jesus Christ, you too have God's love and protection.

Prayer: Dear Lord, I thank You that as Your child, I am under Your eternal love and everlasting protection.

Those who persecute God's people will ultimately
face God's righteous judgment.

Jonah

I know that You are…
One who relents from doing harm. (4:2)

Theme: God's grace to all people
Date written: 780–750 BC
Author: Jonah
Setting: Nineveh

JONAH is the autobiography of a reluctant prophet who tried to flee from God's call on his life. He did not want to preach God's grace and offer of repentance to the godless Assyrians.

LIFE APPLICATION: Don't follow Jonah's example and move through your days with heartless indifference. Instead, follow God's example and develop a genuine love for the lost.

Prayer: Dear Lord, I realize that I cannot escape Your call on my life. I now cease my struggle and submit to Your will.

It is impossible to run away from God.

Micah

*What does the LORD require of you
but to do justly,
to love mercy, and to walk humbly
with your God? (6:8)*

Theme: Divine judgment
Date written: 735–710 BC
Author: Micah
Setting: Samaria and Jerusalem

MICAH begins with judgment for Israel's unfaithfulness and ends on a strong note that the Lord fully intends to fulfill the unconditional promise He made to Israel.

LIFE APPLICATION: God wants to see, in His people, justice and equity tempered with mercy and compassion. Live a godly life and nurture these qualities, and you will please God.

Prayer: God, keep me from practicing my religion only at church. Help me to make it real every day in every way to everyone I meet.

Your religion should result in righteous acts.

Nahum

*The LORD... will not at all
acquit the wicked. (1:3)*

Theme: Consolation
Date written: 690–640 BC
Author: Nahum
Setting: Jerusalem and Nineveh

NAHUM takes us back to Nineveh. About 100 years earlier, God spared the city of Nineveh through the preaching of Jonah. Now, according to Nahum, because of Nineveh's sins, this proud nation will be utterly destroyed.

LIFE APPLICATION: Nahum's message gives you great consolation for today's uncertain times. Remember that God is in control of all events and is able to protect and provide for you.

Prayer: Lord, I thank You for Your Word, which continually gives me assurance of Your love and concern for me.

*The same God who hated evil in the past
still hates evil today.*

Habakkuk

The just shall live by his faith. (2:4)

Theme: Trusting a sovereign God
Date written: 607 BC
Author: Habakkuk
Setting: Judah

HABAKKUK is about trusting a sovereign God. Toward the end of the kingdom of Judah, things went from bad to worse. Judah's unchecked wickedness caused Habakkuk, a little-known prophet and a contemporary of the prophet Jeremiah, to ask "Why?" with regard to God's silence and apparent lack of judgment in purging His covenant people. The core of Habakkuk's message resides in the call to trust God—"The just shall live by his faith" (2:4).

LIFE APPLICATION: Trust the sovereign God who does only what is right. Habakkuk's message calls you to trust the One who is at work in the lives of His people even when it seems like evil has triumphed. Because God is righteous and sovereign, He will not let injustice continue forever. Your responsibility as a believer is to not question God's actions or what looks like a lack of action. Rather, your obligation is to count on God's character. As a believer, you are to steadfastly persevere in faith in spite of what is happening to you or to others.

Prayer: God, Your ways are not my ways. They are beyond my understanding. Help me to trust You...even when life seems impossible and incomprehensible.

Faith is not a one-time act. It's a way of life.

Zephaniah

*Seek the LORD, all you meek
of the earth… (2:3)*

Theme: The "great day of the LORD"
Date written: 635–625 BC
Author: Zephaniah
Setting: Jerusalem

ZEPHANIAH warns of the coming "great day of the LORD" (1:14), a day of judgment, first upon Judah and then upon the rebellious Gentile nations.

LIFE APPLICATION: As a Christian, your future is secure. If you acknowledge Jesus as Lord, you, along with the righteous remnant of Israel, will escape the coming day of the Lord.

Prayer: Lord, no matter how difficult life is now, I look forward to a day of rejoicing when Christ returns to make all things right.

*Live with confidence today, for your future
is secure in Christ.*

Haggai

*Now therefore, thus says the LORD of hosts:
"Consider your ways!" (1:5)*

Theme: Rebuilding the temple
Date written: 520 BC
Author: Haggai
Setting: Judah

HAGGAI is about ordering your priorities. God commissioned Haggai to stir up the Jewish people to not only rebuild the temple, but to reorder their spiritual priorities.

LIFE APPLICATION: Haggai is asking you the same question he asked the people of Israel: "Are you building your own house and allowing God's house and ministries to go neglected?"

Prayer: Dear Lord, help me to review my priorities often and ask, "Are my priorities in line with Yours?"

*God rewards those who put Him first and
seek to do His will.*

Zechariah

I will return to Zion, and
dwell in the midst of Jerusalem. (8:3)

Theme: God's deliverance
Date written: 520–480 BC
Author: Zechariah
Setting: Jerusalem

ZECHARIAH'S ministry overlapped that of Haggai's and the rebuilding of the temple. Zechariah said the rebuilding of the temple was only a first act in the drama of God's history. Next would be the coming of Messiah.

LIFE APPLICATION: Today you can have deliverance—spiritual deliverance—as you put your faith and trust in Jesus as your Savior and your King.

Prayer: Dear Lord, I thank You that You have given me spiritual deliverance from the power of sin through Jesus.

God has promised deliverance and
He keeps His promises.

Malachi

Will a man rob God?
Yet you have robbed Me!
But you say,
"In what way have we robbed You?"
"In tithes and offerings...
Bring all the tithes into the storehouse,
that there may be food in My house,
and try me now in this,"
says the LORD of hosts. (3:8,10)

Theme: Formalism rebuked
Date written: 430 BC
Author: Malachi
Setting: Jerusalem

MALACHI is about faithless ritual. It is the last book of the Old Testament. The people of Israel have returned from captivity and learned their lesson regarding idolatry. The prophet Malachi, like his contemporaries Ezra and Nehemiah, addressed many other evils, such as greed, worldliness, a lack of concern for God's temple and its offerings. The people, including the priests, received the last word of God's judgment for their apathy and ritualism. Another 400 years of silence would go by before John the Baptist would arrive with a message from God of the soon arrival of the Messiah. Interestingly, the message John proclaimed was the same—"Repent" (Matthew 3:2).

LIFE APPLICATION: God's people erred by thinking their halfhearted religious efforts would ensure God's blessings. When God did not bless them, they questioned His character. Does this sound at all familiar? God wants to bless you, but not because of your outward religious service. He wants your heart—your inward, heartfelt obedience. The prophet Samuel said it well: "Does the LORD delight in burnt offerings and sacrifices as much as in obeying the LORD? To obey is better than sacrifice" (1 Samuel 15:22 NIV).

Prayer: Lord, am I just going through the motions in my worship? Check my heart. Apathy toward You precedes faithless worship of You. Renew my passion for You!

God does not bless religious efforts—
He blesses heartfelt obedience.

Matthew

Jesus began to preach and to say,
"Repent, for the kingdom of
heaven is at hand." (4:17)

Theme: The kingdom of God
Date written: AD 60
Author: Matthew (Levi)
Setting: Palestine

MATTHEW is about the arrival of the King. Matthew was a tax collector until Jesus called him to become one of His 12 disciples. Immediately after responding to Christ's call, Matthew held a reception to let everyone know about Jesus and to personally meet Him (Matthew 9:9-13). Later, after Jesus returned to heaven, Matthew wrote to the Jewish Christians who were scattered throughout the Roman Empire. They were beginning to experience persecution, and Matthew wrote to strengthen their faith and give them a tool for evangelizing their Jewish communities. He presented Jesus of Nazareth as Israel's promised Messiah and rightful King.

LIFE APPLICATION: The kingdom of heaven is still being offered to people today, but the price for entry is accepting its King—Jesus Christ—by faith. Only after believing in Jesus alone to save you from your sin will God change you from the inside out to be a citizen of His kingdom. It is a spiritual kingdom now, but when Jesus returns, He will establish His rule on earth.

Are you one of Jesus' subjects? If so, let the whole world know. Like Matthew, be faithful to share the good news of your King with your family, friends, and co-workers. Let them know "The King is coming!"

Prayer: Dear Lord Jesus, I look forward to Your return as King of kings and Lord of lords. May I be faithful to share Your message of salvation with everyone I meet.

Jesus did not preach abstract religion,
but a new way of living.

Mark

The Son of Man did not come to be served,
but to serve,
and to give His life a ransom
for many. (10:45)

Theme: The Suffering Servant
Date written: AD 60
Author: John Mark
Setting: Rome

MARK is about the Suffering Servant. Though John Mark was not an eyewitness of the life of Jesus, he was a close companion of the apostle Peter, who passed on the details of his association with Jesus to Mark. Writing from Rome, Mark targeted Roman believers and presented Jesus as a servant to His fellow man. The book focuses more on Jesus' deeds than His teachings. It demonstrates the humanity of Christ and describes His human emotions, His limitations as a human, and ultimately, His physical death. At the same time, Mark clearly reveals the power and authority of this unique Servant, showing Him as no less than the Son of God, as demonstrated in His resurrection.

LIFE APPLICATION: Like most people, the religious leaders of Jesus' day wanted to be served and rule over others. Yet Jesus taught—and lived—the exact opposite attitude. Real greatness is shown by service and sacrifice. Through Mark's eyes you see Jesus as an active, compassionate, and obedient Servant who constantly ministered to the physical and spiritual needs of others.

Always remember that real greatness is shown by service and sacrifice. Ambition and love of power and position should not be your goal. Instead, seek to be a servant. And who better for you to look to and emulate than the ultimate model of true servanthood, Jesus Christ?

Prayer: Lord, may I always remember that true greatness is not in being served but in serving others. Lead me daily to those whom I can serve in Your name, Lord Jesus.

Jesus came to serve, and He wants you to follow His example.

Luke

*The Son of Man has come to seek and
to save that which was lost. (19:10)*

Theme: The Perfect Man
Date written: AD 60–62
Author: Luke, the beloved physician
Setting: Rome

LUKE is about the Perfect Man. As a doctor and the
only Gentile author of the New Testament, Luke
wrote to give an accurate historical account of the
unique life of Jesus. He wrote to strengthen the
faith of Gentile believers. He described Jesus as
the Perfect Man—the Son of Man—who came
to seek and save sinful men. Luke also showed a
strong interest in how people's lives intersected
with Jesus'. He described Jesus' interactions with
others, in which our Lord disregarded social norms
and religious bigotry. In this way Jesus revealed the
universality of the Christian message.

LIFE APPLICATION: Jesus' love and compassion
should serve as a powerful example as you go about
interacting with other people. For example, you
need to be like the Good Samaritan described by

Jesus in Luke chapter 10—the Samaritan stopped to help a person who was suffering. No, you are not Jesus. But when you perform acts of love and show compassion, you point others to the Spirit of Jesus, who lives in you.

Prayer: Lord Jesus, as I read Your Word, I can see that You expect certain attitudes in my life—attitudes like forgiveness, faithfulness, and thankfulness. Give me strength each day to live out these attitudes and honor Your presence in my life.

Jesus showed compassion for the hurting and the lost, and so should you.

John

*These are written that you may believe that
Jesus is the Christ, the Son of God,
and that believing you may have
life in His name. (20:31)*

Theme: The Son of God
Date written: AD 80–90
Author: John, the disciple whom Jesus loved
Setting: Palestine

JOHN is about the Son of God. The last remaining apostle, John provided a supplement to what was already written about Jesus in the first three Gospel accounts. Genesis began with "In the beginning" God made man in His own image, and John also began with "In the beginning," but said God was made into the image of man, stating, "The Word became flesh" (1:14). John presented the most powerful and direct case for the deity and humanity of the incarnate Son of God. In Jesus, perfect humanity and full deity are fused, making Him the only possible sacrifice for the sins of mankind.

LIFE APPLICATION: Only a fool ignores highway road signs. Likewise, only a spiritual fool ignores the signs in the Bible that lead to salvation. Have you recognized and responded to the signs God has placed before you? John organized his entire Gospel around eight miracles—eight "signs" or proofs of the deity of Jesus. Read the Gospel of John. Ask God for eyes that see the signs. Then embrace their message. Look for the signs that tell you about Jesus Christ—signs that point to the truth that He is the Son of God and the Savior of the world.

Prayer: Lord Jesus, thank You that You have shown me, in Your Word, that You are God in flesh, and that You are the only way, the ultimate truth, and the source of eternal life (John 14:6).

Looking for immortality? Look no further than Jesus.

Acts

*You shall receive power when the Holy Spirit
has come upon you; and you shall be witnesses
to Me in Jerusalem, and in all Judea and
Samaria, and to the end of the earth. (1:8)*

Theme: The spread of the gospel
Date written: AD 60–62
Author: Luke, a Greek physician
Setting: Jerusalem to Rome

ACTS is about the spread of the gospel. This book
is the historical link between the Gospels and the
letters of instruction (the epistles) that make up
the remainder of the New Testament. Acts contains the 30-year history of the church from its
beginning in Jerusalem in Acts 1–2 until chapter 28, where the church and its gospel message
have spread throughout the Roman Empire. Acts
is often referred to as "the Acts of the Holy Spirit,"
for in this book, He is seen working in and through
the apostles.

LIFE APPLICATION: Luke, the author of Acts, was
not a detached bystander reporting historical facts.
No, he was personally involved in the spread of the

gospel, including himself in the action by using the pronoun "we." Do you consider yourself part of the "we" when it comes to sharing the gospel? Are you part of the action, or a mere bystander? Don't stand on the sidelines. Don't be content to watch others share their faith in the risen Christ. Step out in the power of the Holy Spirit. Share what you have seen and heard and learned. Then step back and watch God's Spirit work through your testimony.

Prayer: That You, Holy Spirit, would embolden and empower me to carry out your witness of Jesus to the people around me.

"You will be My witnesses." The early church took these words from Jesus seriously. How about you?

Romans

In [the gospel of Christ] the righteousness of God is revealed from faith to faith; as it is written, "The just shall live by faith." (1:17)

Theme: The righteousness of God
Date written: AD 56–57
Author: Paul
Setting: Corinth (southern Greece)

ROMANS is about the righteousness of God. The apostle Paul wrote this letter to a church in Rome he had never visited. He wrote to introduce himself so the people could pray for him, encourage him, and help him with his future plans for ministry. Paul also taught his new friends in Rome about the righteousness that comes from God— the great truth of the gospel of grace. This letter is the most forceful, logical, and articulate treatise on salvation ever penned, and has influenced the history of Christianity more than any other epistle.

LIFE APPLICATION: All men and women are sinners—and that includes you and me. Your sin separates you from a holy God. But God graciously extends an offer of salvation to you and all who place their faith and trust in Jesus. Have you accepted God's offer of salvation? The righteousness of God is a gift received only by faith, not earned by your works. In fact, everything you receive as a Christian, whether spiritual or physical, is a work of God's grace. If you have received God's grace, then you possess the righteousness of God in Christ. This inward change should produce a corresponding outward change. Therefore, God now empowers and expects you to live a righteous life that honors Him.

Prayer: Thank You, dear Father, for my salvation through Your gift of grace. Help me show my devotion for this gift by faithfully serving You and my fellow believers.

Faithfulness in the little things will prepare you for greater tasks from God.

1 Corinthians

Whether you eat or drink,
or whatever you do,
do all to the glory of God. (10:31)

Theme: Christian conduct
Date written: AD 55
Author: Paul
Setting: Ephesus (modern Turkey)

1 CORINTHIANS is about Christian conduct. Using his God-given power and authority as an apostle (one sent by God as His spokesman), Paul wrote this first of two letters to believers in Corinth. This letter was filled with many exhortations for the Corinthian believers to act like Christians. Their most serious problem was worldliness. They were unwilling to let go of the culture around them. In this letter, Paul firmly addressed their deplorable conduct and answered some important questions asked by representatives from the Corinthian church.

LIFE APPLICATION: Whether you realize it or not, your behavior is being influenced by today's culture. As a Christian, the challenge for you is to keep the world from filling your mind with wrong thoughts, which in turn will result in wrong actions. What is the answer to this problem? Just as Paul attempted to correct the Corinthians through proper teaching, you can make sure your behavior is correct by developing a proper understanding of God's Word. With God's help, you can keep your behavior in line with His standards. That's why you want to commit yourself to reading, studying, and obeying His Word.

Prayer: Lord, help me to not be attached to this world, and to remember that earth is not my home. I am just passing through on my way to heaven!

Though you are in the world,
you are not to be tied to
the world.

2 Corinthians

We do not preach ourselves,
but Christ Jesus the Lord,
and ourselves your bondservants
for Jesus' sake. (4:5)

Theme: Paul's defense of his apostleship
Date written: AD 56
Author: Paul
Setting: Philippi (on the way to Corinth)

2 CORINTHIANS is about Paul's defense of his apostleship. As Paul traveled toward Corinth for Ephesus, where he had written 1 Corinthians, Titus, one of Paul's young disciples, intercepted him and reported that the Corinthians had repented of their resistance against Paul and his teaching. With great joy, Paul wrote a follow-up letter, 2 Corinthians. Then he sent it on ahead by the hand of Titus. In this second letter, Paul defended his life and ministry, and expressed his ongoing concerns about new threats and rebellious attitudes.

LIFE APPLICATION: As you seek to live for Christ, like Paul, you will probably be maligned, misunderstood, undermined, and falsely accused. When that happens, do as Paul did—look to Jesus. Recall who you are in Him and what He has done in and through you. Rather than dread the trials that are coming your way, take courage in the fact that God is faithful. The strength He gives to you is sufficient for any trial you are facing or will face in the future. After all, He is the "God of all comfort" (2 Corinthians 1:3), and He promises to comfort you in all your tribulation.

Prayer: Lord, I realize that I am not immune from trials, and that living as a Christian means suffering. In times of trouble, help me to look up to You who made heaven and earth (Psalm 121:1-2)!

Trials are used by God to teach dependence on His unlimited strength rather than on your limited strength.

Galatians

*Stand fast therefore in the liberty by which
Christ has made us free,
and do not be entangled again
with a yoke of bondage. (5:1)*

Theme: Freedom in Christ
Date written: AD 49
Author: Paul
Setting: Antioch

GALATIANS is about justification by faith apart from the works of the law. While ministering in his home church at Antioch, Paul was shocked by some distressing news. He feared that the churches in southern Galatia, which he had established on his first missionary journey, had abandoned the pure gospel of faith in Christ alone for salvation. He sent this urgent letter to defend this key point of the doctrine of salvation. His letter had three purposes:

1. To defend his apostolic authority, which affirmed his gospel message.
2. To use the Mosaic Law to teach the principles of justification by faith alone.

There is nothing you can do to gain favor with God. Salvation is through God's grace alone.

3. To show that liberty from the law does not excuse sinful behavior.

LIFE APPLICATION: As a Christian, you are no longer under the rules and judgments of the Old Testament law. Christ has set you free from religious works. Yet with freedom comes responsibility. You are responsible to serve your Savior and do His will. And you are not free to disobey Christ's standards. Therefore, as Paul wrote, you are not to "use liberty as an opportunity for the flesh, but through love serve one another" (Galatians 5:13).

Prayer: Dear Father, I thank You that my salvation is not based on my own merit, but on the sinless merit of the Lord Jesus Christ, who alone makes possible everything I am and can be as a Christian.

God's love and His gift of salvation are given to you by God's grace— not earned by your works.

Ephesians

Blessed be the God and Father
of our Lord Jesus Christ,
who has blessed us with
every spiritual blessing in
the heavenly places in Christ. (1:3)

Theme: Blessings in Christ
Date written: AD 60–62
Author: Paul
Setting: A Roman prison

EPHESIANS is about blessings in Christ. Paul wrote this epistle to the Ephesian church to make its members more aware of their spiritual resources. In the first three chapters he explained that their resources come from their relationship with Christ and their position in Him. Then in the last three chapters he encouraged his readers to draw upon those resources so they could live in a victorious manner. Put another way, the first half of the book of Ephesians describes a believer's wealth in Christ, and the last half challenges a believer to live out his or her faith.

LIFE APPLICATION: Everyone who has trusted in Christ possesses an endless supply of spiritual blessings. Unfortunately, most believers act as though they are spiritual beggars and live in defeat. Are you unaware of the resources that are yours in Christ, and therefore failing to appropriate those divine resources? Do you understand what resources you possess in Christ? If not, Ephesians will help you find out. If you do know what your resources are, then start or continue to "walk worthy of the calling with which you are called" (4:1).

Prayer: Lord, to ensure I experience spiritual victory, help me remember to use the spiritual resources You have given me, including the spiritual armor described in Ephesians 6:10-17.

God has given you the tools you need to
fight against the enemy.

Philippians

Rejoice in the Lord always.
Again I will say, rejoice! (4:4)

Theme: The joy-filled life
Date written: AD 62
Author: Paul
Setting: Prison

PHILIPPIANS focuses on living a joy-filled life. When Paul wrote, "Rejoice in the Lord always" (4:4), he was not sitting in comfort or in pleasant surroundings. Instead, he was a captive in a Roman prison. Yet Paul could rejoice even while in prison because of his passion for knowing Jesus Christ more and more. This is the secret of a joyful Christian life. True joy is not based on circumstances, but in the confidence that comes from a relationship with Jesus Christ.

LIFE APPLICATION: Everyone wants to be happy, so they pack their lives with spending money, traveling, and experiencing new and exciting activities. But this kind of happiness depends on positive circumstances. What happens when your circumstances aren't so positive? Often your happiness disappears and despair sets in. In bold contrast to happiness stands God's brand of joy. True joy comes from knowing Christ personally and from depending on His strength and provision rather than your own. Your circumstances may change, but your joy stands grounded in knowing Jesus is at work in your life.

Prayer: Lord Jesus, help me not shy away from the difficulties that life presents, for as I demonstrate Your joy in the midst of these trials, I am exposing the world to Your amazing grace.

God never promised His children
a pain-free life, but He does promise
a pain-free eternity.

Colossians

*In Him dwells all the fullness
of the Godhead bodily;
and you are complete in Him... (2:9-10)*

Theme: The supremacy of Christ
Date written: AD 60–61
Author: Paul
Setting: Prison

COLOSSIANS is about the supremacy of Christ. The apostle Paul had never been to the church in Colosse. However, a man named Epaphras came to Rome to visit Paul and to report his concerns about a heretical philosophy that was being taught in Colosse. Paul immediately penned this letter to warn his readers against this heresy that was devaluing Christ's sufficiency. Paul wrote to give the believers a proper understanding of Christ's attributes and His accomplishments.

LIFE APPLICATION: From the time of the writing of Colossians until today, the world has been trying to devalue the importance of Christ. If He is less than supreme, then submission to Him is optional. Yet the book of Colossians says Christ is supreme, and therefore submission to His commands is not optional. Christ is supreme, and your commitment to Him should be supreme. Is Christ dominant in your life? If not, you can submit to His authority right now. In response, He will provide the power to transform every area of your life, including your home and your job. Christ is sufficient for your every area of need.

Prayer: Dear Father in heaven, I thank You that I am totally sufficient in Christ and I have no need for special knowledge or unique religious experiences. Christ is sufficient for all my insufficiencies.

*The Christian life means
putting off the character of the world and
putting on the character of Christ.*

1 Thessalonians

If we believe that Jesus died and rose again,
even so God will bring with Him
those who sleep in Jesus. (4:14)

Theme: Concern for the church
Date written: AD 51
Author: Paul
Setting: Corinth

1 THESSALONIANS highlights Paul's concern for the church. During his brief stay in Thessalonica, he had taught the Christians that Christ's second coming would be the culmination of redemptive history. Therefore, the church was living in expectation of the soon return of Christ. Paul later received word that some of the believers in Thessalonica who had lost loved ones and friends were wondering, "Will these departed souls miss Christ's return?" Paul wrote to inform them that the deceased believers had not missed out on Jesus' return, and assured them that even dead believers would participate in Christ's second coming.

LIFE APPLICATION: No one knows the time of Christ's return. However, one day all believers, both those who are alive and those who have died, will be united with Christ. Daily anticipation of His return should comfort you as you deal with your everyday difficulties. Knowing that Christ will return should also motivate you to share the gospel with others. Your testimony, or account of how Christ changed your life, is a powerful witnessing tool. Beyond that, live a holy and productive life. Live each day in expectation, and don't be caught unprepared.

Prayer: Lord, is today the day of Your return? May I live today as if eternity with Christ will begin today.

The promised return of Christ should motivate you toward daily holy living.

2 Thessalonians

The Lord is faithful,
who will establish you and guard you
from the evil one. (3:3)

Theme: Living in hope
Date written: AD 52
Author: Paul
Setting: Corinth

2 THESSALONIANS calls Christians to live in hope. As he did in 1 Thessalonians, Paul commended the people in the church for their faith in Christ. Unfortunately, some of them had misunderstood his teaching about Christ's return and had stopped working because they thought Christ would come very soon. Others viewed their continued persecution as a sign that the last days were at hand. Paul responded to the incorrect thinking of these two groups: To the one, he said to start working. To those who believed that "the day of the Lord" had already come, he warned them that mass apostasy and rebellion would occur before that day. Paul then consoled them in their suffering and persecution by reminding them that when Christ returns, He will reward the faithful and punish the wicked.

LIFE APPLICATION: This letter from Paul should help you to not become discouraged or afraid when you are persecuted or see evil on the increase. God is always in control, no matter how desperate things look or become. He has a plan for your future, and this hope should give you the strength and assurance you need to keep moving forward instead of putting life on hold and doing nothing while you wait on Christ's return. Paul's encouragement to you is to stand firm, keep working, keep doing good, and keep waiting for Christ.

Prayer: Dear heavenly Father, I take great confidence and hope in the fact that no matter what lies ahead, You hold the future. Give me the strength to face each day with that assurance.

Despair sees no hope, while hope sees no despair.

1 Timothy

If I am delayed, I write so that you may know how you ought to conduct yourself in the house of God, which is the church of the living God... (3:15)

Theme: Instructions for a young disciple
Date written: AD 64
Author: Paul
Setting: Macedonia/Philippi

1 TIMOTHY delivers instructions to a young disciple. At the time Paul wrote this letter, Timothy had been a close disciple of Paul's for some 15 years. Timothy was serving as pastor of the church at Ephesus, and Paul hoped to eventually return in person, but in the meantime, Paul wrote this letter to give Timothy some practical advice about his conduct, about the importance of choosing qualified leaders, and to deliver a warning about the problem of false doctrine and false teachers.

LIFE APPLICATION: Do you know the truths in God's Word well enough to spot a false teacher or false teaching? Are you prepared to defend the Christian faith with your present level of biblical knowledge? If so, follow Paul's example and find younger-in-the-faith Christians like Timothy and begin mentoring them. If not, follow the example of Timothy and gain wisdom by learning from a more mature Christian.

Prayer: Lord Jesus, thank You for this model of discipleship between Paul and Timothy. There is so much I don't know about how to live the Christian life. Lead me to a more mature believer so I can imitate their godly life.

Study your Bible for the truth so you can spot error.

2 Timothy

Be diligent to present yourself approved to God,
a worker who does not need to be ashamed,
rightly dividing the word of truth. (2:15)

Theme: A charge to faithful ministry
Date written: AD 67
Author: Paul
Setting: Rome

2 TIMOTHY issues a charge to faithful ministry. If you were told you were going to die in the near future, what information would you want to pass on, and who would you want to receive it? That was Paul's situation in 2 Timothy. He was on death row awaiting his execution for preaching the gospel of Christ. The letter of 2 Timothy is Paul's last will and testament. Of all the people Paul had known over the years, he chose to write one last letter to his spiritual son in the faith. Paul wrote to comfort, encourage, and motivate Timothy to continue in faithful ministry.

LIFE APPLICATION: How does Paul's utter disregard for himself while facing death strike you? Are you so busy focusing on yourself and your perceived needs that you are failing to notice the truly needy people around you?

Take a good look outside yourself. You are sure to find plenty of desperate people who could use a helping hand or a word of encouragement, especially a message from God's Word delivered to them...by you.

Prayer: Lord, as I look into the mirror of my soul, do I see a person who is preoccupied with self, or one who is noticing the needs of others? Help me make the changes necessary to look beyond myself, starting with my family!

Scripture is your best tool for encouraging others. Give "a word in season to him who is weary" (Isaiah 50:4).

Titus

*As for you, speak the things
which are proper for sound doctrine. (2:1)*

Theme: A manual of conduct
Date written: AD 62–64
Author: Paul
Setting: Macedonia

TITUS is a manual of conduct. In the book of Titus, Paul gave personal encouragement and counsel to the young pastor, Titus, who was facing opposition from ungodly men within the newly formed churches on the island of Crete. Paul affirmed that sound teaching at all levels would help keep the believers unified against opposition both within the church and before the world. Paul wrote to Titus about equipping the people to live as effective witnesses for Jesus Christ. He then gave instructions on how young-in-the-faith believers were to conduct themselves before a pagan society that was eager to criticize this new religion, Christianity.

LIFE APPLICATION: Whether in AD 62 or today, the corporate witness of a church must have a unified message. There cannot be dissension and strife.

Have you recently thought about your conduct both inside and outside the church? Ask God to give you insight into your behavior at church and in public. Realize that your godly behavior helps promote unity within your church, and your good works outside the church are a beacon of light that helps lead others to the Savior.

Prayer: Lord if my church is to glorify You before a watching world, I need to ensure that my conduct promotes unity rather than disunity.

> *Your conduct exposes your true*
> *spiritual condition.*

Philemon

If then you count me as a partner, receive him as you would me. (verse 17)

Theme: Forgiveness
Date written: AD 60–62
Author: Paul
Setting: Prison

PHILEMON is the shortest of the four prison epistles. In it, Paul appeals to his friend, Philemon, not to punish his runaway slave, Onesimus, but to forgive and restore him as a new Christian brother.

LIFE APPLICATION: Forgiveness is a foundational aspect of Christianity. On the basis of the forgiveness Christ has shown to you, you can and should be willing to forgive others.

Prayer: Lord, is there someone who, until now, I have been unwilling to forgive? Examine my heart that I may forgive as I have been forgiven!

A forgiven Christian is a forgiving Christian.

Hebrews

Seeing then that we have a great High Priest
who has passed through the heavens,
Jesus the Son of God,
let us hold fast our confession. (4:14)

Theme: The superiority of Christ
Date written: AD 67–69
Author: Unknown
Setting: A community of Jewish Christians

HEBREWS focuses on the superiority of Christ. The book of Hebrews was written to Jews who had accepted Jesus as the Messiah, but were drifting back into their old familiar religious ways, especially as persecution mounted against Christians. Authored by an unknown writer, Hebrews presents the overarching message that Christianity is superior to all other religious systems, including the Jewish religion with its Old Testament rituals and sacrifices. No religious system is necessary because Christ is superior, and He is completely sufficient in Himself for salvation.

LIFE APPLICATION: Faith is confident trust in God and the salvation He provides in His Son Jesus, who is the only one who can save you from sin. If you trust in Jesus Christ completely for your salvation, He will transform you completely. This transformation and subsequent growth enables you to face trials, stay true to God when you are being persecuted, and build your character. Your Savior is superior, the faith placed in your Savior is superior, and your final victory through your Savior is assured.

Prayer: Dear Father, I thank You that my faith is based on my confident trust in You and the salvation You provide in Your Son, the Lord Jesus Christ.

Spiritual maturity is not the result of salvation,
but the response to salvation.

James

*Faith by itself, if it does not
have works, is dead. (2:17)*

Theme: Genuine faith
Date written: AD 44–49
Author: James
Setting: Jerusalem

JAMES is about genuine faith. The book of James
was written by James, the half-brother of Jesus
and leader of the Jerusalem church. James was the
earliest of the New Testament epistles or letters.
In a style similar to that found in the Old Testament book of Proverbs, James presented a series
of tests by which a person's faith in Christ can be
measured. If real change is absent, then readers are
exhorted to examine their faith to make sure they
are not exhibiting symptoms of dead faith—which
is really no faith!

LIFE APPLICATION: The book of James is a reminder that genuine faith transforms lives. Your
faith in Christ must be put into action. It is easy to
say you have faith, but true faith will produce lov-
ing actions toward others. Your faith must not be

mere head knowledge, but it must also be lived out by heart actions. The proof that your faith is genuine is a changed life manifested by practical Christian living. James 1:19 says believers are to be "swift to hear, slow to speak, slow to wrath." You cannot get much more practical than that! Genuine faith will produce genuine changes in your life.

Prayer: Lord, may I be a doer of Your Word and not just a listener. Help me take what I know of Your Word and start living it out in my life—today!

God is not a respecter of persons, and you should not be either.

1 Peter

To this you were called,
because Christ also suffered for us,
leaving us an example,
that you should follow His steps. (2:21)

Theme: Responding to suffering
Date written: AD 64–65
Author: Peter
Setting: Rome

1 PETER addresses how to respond to suffering.
Peter composed this letter to Christians who were
experiencing persecution because of their faith in
Christ. He wrote to comfort them by reminding
them of their salvation and their hope of eternal life.
He also reminded his readers that God was using
all that was going on in their lives—including their
struggles—to produce strength of character, which
always brings glory to God. He challenged them to
realize that those who suffer for their faith become
partners with Christ in His suffering.

LIFE APPLICATION: Today you may be one of the
many Christians around the world who is suffering for what you believe. But all Christians should

expect persecution, for Jesus said, "In the world you will have tribulation" (John 16:33). If your faith is seen by others, you can expect some ridicule and rejection. But Peter said you don't have to be terrified by such treatment. You need to see each confrontation as an opportunity to have your faith refined and strengthened. As you face persecution and suffering, remember Peter's words: "For to this you were called, because Christ also suffered for us, leaving us an example, that you should follow His steps" (1 Peter 2:21).

Prayer: Lord, Your Word says that persecution comes to the godly. Help me live godly so that I can face persecution victoriously as Christ did. Help me to rely fully on You.

You shouldn't be surprised when persecution comes. It's a given for those who faithfully follow Jesus.

2 Peter

*We have the prophetic word confirmed, which
you do well to heed as a light that shines
in a dark place, until the day dawns and
the morning star rises in your hearts... (1:19)*

Theme: Warning against false teachers
Date written: AD 67–68
Author: Peter
Setting: A Roman prison

2 PETER contains a warning against false teachers. About three years after he wrote his first letter, the apostle Peter wrote a second letter from his prison cell. In the letter, he expressed alarm about the false teachers who had invaded the churches in Asia Minor. Peter said these internal attacks by the enemy were coming as a result of stagnation and heresy. In Peter's mind, the cure for these two problems was growth in the grace and knowledge of Christ (3:18). The best antidote for error is a maturing understanding of the truth.

LIFE APPLICATION: Warnings come in many forms—lights, signs, sounds, smells, and the written word. No person who values their physical life would fail to respond to one or all of these forms of warning. As you read your Bible, are you paying attention to God's warnings of spiritual danger? Heed 2 Peter 3:18 and grow in the grace and knowledge of Jesus. Your growth combats spiritual laziness and deception by the enemy. Spiritual growth will keep you faithful and give you the discernment to defend against the wiles and ways of Satan and his false teachers.

Prayer: Dear God, may I be faithful to read my Bible so that I will grow spiritually and develop the discernment needed to respond to the warnings You want me to heed.

The best way to recognize spiritual error
is to know spiritual truth as revealed
in the Bible.

1 John

*That which we have seen and
heard we declare to you,
that you also may have fellowship with us;
and truly our fellowship is with the Father
and with His Son Jesus Christ. (1:3)*

Theme: Fellowship with God
Date written: AD 90
Author: John
Setting: Ephesus

1 JOHN encourages fellowship with God. By the time this epistle was written, some 50 years had passed since Jesus physically walked the earth. Most of the eyewitnesses of Christ's ministry had died, but John was still alive to testify about Jesus. In simple terms, John described what it means to have fellowship with God. At the same time, he warned that false teachers had entered the churches, denying that Jesus had actually come in the flesh. These teachers openly rejected the incarnation of Christ, and John wrote from personal experience to correct this error.

LIFE APPLICATION: Basic to the Christian faith is the truth that Jesus alone was qualified to offer up the perfect sacrifice for our sins—His body. As God in human flesh, He and He alone was qualified to satisfy God the Father's penalty for sin. John painted a clear picture of Jesus the Christ, the Son of God, God in human flesh. Do you believe in Jesus as the Son of God? If you do, John says, "This is the testimony: that God has given us eternal life, and this life is in His Son. He who has the Son has life" (1 John 5:11-12).

Prayer: Lord, a mark of my fellowship with You is my love for Your Son and my love for others. Help me daily to affirm that love by being obedient to the commands of Scripture.

Love is a mark of your fellowship with God.

2 John

*If anyone comes to you and does not bring
this doctrine, do not receive him... (verse 10)*

Theme: Christian discernment
Date written: AD 90–95
Author: John
Setting: Ephesus

2 JOHN was written to a specific woman who
may have unknowingly shown hospitality to false
teachers. John feared these deceivers were taking
advantage of her and warned her not to show hospitality to them.

LIFE APPLICATION: John's concern is appropriate for us today. Your Christian hospitality is to
be practiced with discernment. Scripture advises
you to avoid those who do not abide by the teachings of Christ.

Prayer: Realizing that false teachers are very decep-
tive, Lord, give me discernment to make sure their
lives and teaching match Scripture.

*Walking in obedience to truth is to be
the habit of your life.*

3 John

*Beloved, you do faithfully whatever you do
for the brethren and for strangers... (verse 5)*

Theme: Christian hospitality
Date written: AD 90–95
Author: John
Setting: Ephesus

3 JOHN contains three messages: Gaius is commended for his ministry of hospitality; Diotrephes is condemned because he would not show hospitality; Demetrius is congratulated because he did what was right and showed hospitality.

LIFE APPLICATION: John's short letter is a great reminder of the constructive role of hospitality in the church...and the destructive power of pride in a church leader.

Prayer: May I take time today to pray for and encourage Christian workers so they don't grow weary in their service.

*Realize that Christian teachers, leaders, and
missionaries need your support.*

Jude

*Beloved, while I was very diligent to write
to you concerning our common salvation,
I found it necessary to write to you exhorting
you to contend earnestly for
the faith... (verse 3)*

Theme: Contending for the faith
Date written: AD 68–69
Author: Jude
Setting: Jerusalem

JUDE is about contending for the faith. As the half-brother of Jesus, and because he was an eyewitness of Jesus' life, ministry, and resurrection, Jude had a burning passion for the salvation that comes in Christ. As he wrote, however, he raised a matter that was of intense concern to him. He saw the threat of heretical teachers in the church and wanted to alert Christians about the proper way to respond to them. Jude sought to motivate his readers to wake up from their complacency and take action against false teachers.

LIFE APPLICATION: Today, as in centuries past, false teachers have infiltrated our churches, Bible colleges, and Christian institutions. God's truths, as found in the Bible, are of infinite value, and they are under attack. What price are you willing to pay to defend God's truth? Are you ready to stand with Jude and "contend earnestly for the faith which was once for all delivered to the saints" (verse 3)? If so, then you stand with Jude in the long line of faithful Christian soldiers who have answered the call and are fighting the good fight of faith.

Prayer: Lord, help me see the urgency of the hour and realize that Your Word is under attack. May I too stand with others who will faithfully point to Christ with their words and their conduct.

Complacency is not an option for Christians.
You are to earnestly contend for the faith!

Revelation

The Revelation of Jesus Christ,
which God gave Him to show His servants—
things which must shortly take place.
And He sent and signified it by His angel
to His servant John… (1:1)

Theme: The unveiling of Jesus Christ
Date written: AD 94–96
Author: John
Setting: Isle of Patmos

REVELATION spotlights the unveiling of Jesus Christ. The word "revelation" (1:1) means "to uncover or to reveal." God began the process of revealing Himself to mankind from the very first verse of the Bible in Genesis. Now the book of Revelation shows that the climax of revelation is coming: God's promises of Christ's return are about to be fulfilled. Jesus, the Suffering Servant and the ultimate revelation of God, is going to return to earth in all His glory and power. He will conquer all who have and would defy Him and rescue His chosen people. Eventually history will be complete. Time will cease, and all creation will again be enveloped into eternity.

LIFE APPLICATION: In the book of Revelation, the beginning signs that the King is coming in judgment are unfolding. For any believer who is compromising and getting involved with the world, this book is a challenge to refocus on Jesus and His will. For any who have become complacent, this book should serve as motivation to a higher level of diligence while watching and waiting for the Lord. The Lord is coming. Are you prepared?

> God controls all people and events.
> ...This should give you confidence for the future.
>
> God's justice and righteousness will prevail in the end.
> ...This should give you encouragement for each day.
>
> God will one day give you perfection and glory in heaven.
> ...This should give you hope for eternity.
>
> God is worthy of worship at all times.
> ...This should give you reason to praise Him—now!

Other Books by Jim George

A Man After God's Own Heart

A Man After God's Own Heart Devotional

A Husband After God's Own Heart

A Leader After God's Own Heart

The Man Who Makes a Difference

One-Minute Insights for Men

A Young Man After God's Own Heart

A Young Man's Guide to Discovering His Bible

A Young Man's Guide to
Making Right Choices

The 50 Most Important
Teachings of the Bible

The Bare Bones Bible® Handbook

The Bare Bones Bible® Handbook for Teens

10 Minutes to Knowing the Men
and Women of the Bible

Know Your Bible from A to Z

A Boy After God's Own Heart

A Boy's Guide to Discovering His Bible

A Boy's Guide to Making Really Good Choices

You Always Have a Friend
in Jesus for Boys

God Loves His Precious Children
(coauthored with Elizabeth George)

God's Wisdom for Little Boys
(coauthored with Elizabeth George)